Written and compiled by
Simon Brett and Richard Berndes

TOP THAT!™

Copyright © 2004 Top That! Publishing plc
Top That! Publishing,
25031 W. Avenue Stanford
Suite #60, Valencia
CA 91355
www.topthatpublishing.com

Contents

3

Introduction

Wherever drinking games originated, they now constitute a thriving area of social culture, being played in bars, homes, and at universities throughout the land.

This book collects together an eclectic selection of the finest available games for your edification and enjoyment.

It includes classic card games such as High or Low and Pyramid, which are easy to play and have the potential to last for hours.

For the risk-takers amongst you, dice games such as Sixes can inject a note of chance into what might be an otherwise predictable evening.

Couch potatoes might like to know that several of our games require only a TV, an appropriate video (or DVD), and a full glass.

I Have Never presents you with the opportunity to reveal your secrets and hear the secrets of others.

To strike a note of caution: please be careful. All these games can be played with soft drinks, but it would be naive to suggest that you refrain from using alcohol altogether!

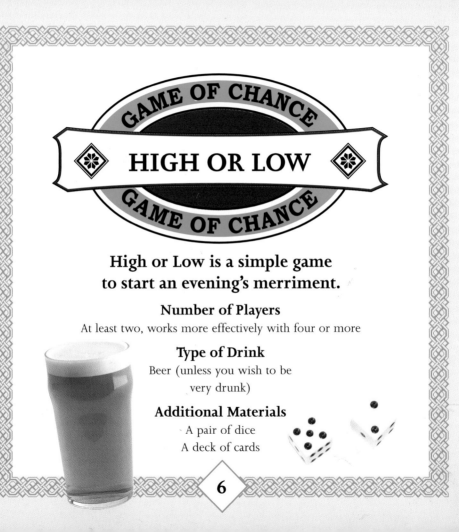

GAME OF CHANCE

HIGH OR LOW

**High or Low is a simple game
to start an evening's merriment.**

Number of Players
At least two, works more effectively with four or more

Type of Drink
Beer (unless you wish to be
very drunk)

Additional Materials
A pair of dice
A deck of cards

6

Rules of the game

The first player is dealt a card, and asked to guess whether the next card will be of higher or lower value (aces high).

If they are correct, they are asked to guess again. Play continues in this fashion, with a player being allowed to pass the stack after they have taken at least three cards.

As soon as someone guesses incorrectly, however, that person is required to drink a measure (a finger of beer, for example) for each card showing. Once he or she has drunk, play starts again with a fresh stack of cards.

As play continues, of course, the stakes become higher, so a smart (or simply vindictive) player will build up a stack before passing it on to their neighbor.

If a player is dealt a card of equal value to the one at the top of their stack, that card is added to the pile and the player guesses again. An equal value card, then, is discounted as a guess but counted when the time comes for someone to drink.

GAME OF SKILL

HOLE IN ONE

GAME OF SKILL

Hole in One is a game for the steady of hand, brave of heart, and strong of stomach.

Number of Players
The larger the number, the smaller the chance that you will be consuming a drink filled with ash

Type of Drink
Anything that comes in a tall glass

Additional Materials
Tissues • Cigarettes • Rubber bands
A medium-sized coin

Rules of the game

A tissue is placed over the top of a full glass, and secured by a rubber band. The coin is placed on top of the contraption.

Players take it in turns to burn a hole in the tissue with a cigarette, and each hole must be at least as wide as the cigarette itself.

This rule is enforced to prevent people from making minuscule holes and claiming that they are playing the game properly.

Finally, one person will cause the tissue to collapse, spilling the coin into the glass.

This person is required to drink the ash-infested beer and recover the coin.

What's more, the same person is expected to buy the next drink, though they are also offered the privilege of resetting the game and taking the first (comparatively safe) turn at burning the new tissue.

GAME OF SPEED

NAME GAME

GAME OF SPEED

**Simple to play, but offers the
potential for hours of fun and frolics.**

Number of Players
Works most effectively in a group of six or more

Type of Drink
Whatever you feel like, though can be
deadly if played with spirits

Additional Materials
A spirit of friendly bonhomie
Knowledge of famous folk

Rules of the game

To begin the game, a group of people sit in a circle and one person calls out the direction in which they wish play to move and the name of a famous person. A possible opening, then, would be: "To my right, Stan Laurel."

The next player is required to call out the name of a second famous person, whose first name begins with the same letter as the previous famous person's surname.

In theory it sounds complicated, but in practice it is simple. A potential follow-up to "Stan Laurel" would be "Leonardo DiCaprio."

Play continues in this fashion, with players merrily naming famous people.

The reason the game is sometimes known as Drink While You Think, however, is that each player is expected to call out a famous person's name immediately. If there is any delay, the player drinks until they are able to think of an appropriate name, whereupon play continues.

There are a couple of rules which spice the game up.

Firstly, if someone calls out the name of a person whose first name and surname start with the same letter, the direction of play reverses. If, in response to "Leonardo DiCaprio," the next player said "David Duchovny," play would revert back to the person who called out "Leonardo DiCaprio."

Also, if someone calls the name of a person who is identified by a single name, for example, "Madonna," play continues in the same direction but skips a player. These rules sometimes lead to people engaging each other in a battle of wits, turning the direction of play back and forth.

Some people object to the inclusion of cartoon characters and fictional folk in this game, and others include rules such as a ban on naming football players, in order to keep things fair when playing this game with football enthusiasts. All such rules are at the discretion of whoever is playing the game.

SIXES

GAME OF CHANCE
GAME OF CHANCE

Sixes is a very simple game of chance.

Number of Players
Works best with four or more

Type of Drink
Anything will do, but a mixture works well

Additional Materials
A die
A selection of six glasses of differing sizes

Rules of the game

Six glasses are arranged appropriately, in a circle or a line, and numbered.

Each person takes turns rolling the die, with the number that they roll corresponding to a glass.

If the glass is empty, the person is entitled to fill it with as much as they like of whatever drink takes their fancy. If the glass contains liquid, they are expected to drain it.

Sixes offers the potential for some spectacular cruelty, for example one person might choose to fill a tall glass with a spirit. However, because it is a game of chance, there is always the possibility that such tactics will backfire horribly, forcing the person who filled the glass to drink its contents.

Another consideration is that the mixing of drinks possible in sixes could lead to horrendous hangovers, so some folk might prefer to stick to a single type of drink.

The game can be varied by using a different number of glasses and a die with a corresponding number of sides.

TV CHARACTERS

A great game for couch potatoes.

Number of Players

Ideally, as many as there are characters who appear
regularly in your chosen TV program.

Type of Drink

Beer or soft drink, otherwise you may
be waking up in hospital

Additional Materials

A working television
A video of your chosen program or
access to TV network showing it

16

Rules of the game

This game is very simple indeed. A program (*Dawson's Creek*, for example) is selected, and each player chooses a character to represent themselves. In the example above, one person would be Dawson, another Pacey, someone else Joey etc.

During the show, each player drinks while their adopted character is on screen. This can require serious drinking ability, or a lot of ineffectual slurping.

If a player's character is mentioned while off screen, the player is expected to drink one sip, or finger, of their drink. It's as simple as that.

Other potential choices with which to play this game include shows such as *Buffy the Vampire Slayer* or *The Sopranos* (though whoever is the main character may need to be a drinker of professional status) and soap operas or ensemble pieces such as *ER*.

A psychological aside:
the character chosen by each player
can reveal a lot about how they
see themselves!

GAME OF SPEED

❖ DROWN THE CLOWN ❖

GAME OF SPEED

A card game with a kick.

Number of Players
The more the merrier

Type of Drink
Works with beer, wine, or spirits

Additional Materials
Several decks of cards, reduced to include only
jacks, queens, kings, and aces

Rules of the game

To begin this game, the cards are shuffled and each player is dealt one card.

On the count of three, each player flips over their card and scans the other cards looking for one which matches theirs (hence the need for several packs of cards).

A player who spots a matching card is required to point at the player who was dealt the matching card and unleash a rousing shout of "Clown," before the same is said to him or her.

Whichever player yells "Clown" first escapes a forfeit; the player who is "clowned" pays by

drinking whatever quantity is deemed appropriate.

If anyone makes a mistake, by pointing at someone who holds a different card or by saying anything other than "Clown," they are required to pay a drinking fine.

This game can be particularly fun if played in a large group, when several matches come up at once.

GAME OF SKILL

BEER PONG

❋ ❋

GAME OF SKILL

Combine beer with sport!

Number of Players
Two at a time, with
opportunities to alternate

Type of Drink
Well, beer...

Additional Materials
A good-sized table or suitable flat surface
Table tennis balls
Plastic cups

Rules of the game

The game begins with each player filling their selection of plastic cups about one third full of beer and arranging them in a triangle on their side of the table. Six cups works well, but ten is better for hardened drinkers.

Player one takes two shots at throwing (or bouncing) a table tennis ball into any of player two's cups.

Player two is expected to drain any cups which player one lands a table tennis ball in: if player one is successful with both throws, they are rewarded with a bonus shot.

Subsequently, play reverses; player two has two attempts at landing a table tennis ball in player one's cups, with the possibility of a bonus throw if they are successful twice.

Play continues until one of the players is out of beer, at which point the winner is declared and the loser is expected to drain all the winner's remaining cups.

A "winner stays on" system can be initiated, testing the winner's mettle further and giving the loser an opportunity to sober up.

GAME OF CHANCE

❖ 7 11 DOUBLES ❖

GAME OF CHANCE

A game ideal for big drinkers.

Number of Players
Four to six, ideally

Type of Drink
Lager, beer etc.

Additional Materials
A table • Two dice • A tall glass

Rules of the game

Play begins with players seated around the table, with one player holding the dice.

This player rolls the dice in an attempt to roll a seven, an eleven, or a double. If the player fails, the dice are passed to the left. If the player succeeds, the dice are left where they lie and the successful roller selects an opponent to challenge in a Herculean test of drinking ability and dice-rolling skill.

In order to set up the challenge, the glass is filled with an appropriate quantity of whatever beverage is being used. The drinker is aiming to gulp down the entire contents of the glass before the roller throws a seven, an eleven, or a double. The roller, of course, is aiming to throw a seven, an eleven, or a double before the drinker empties their glass.

If the roller is successful, the challenge is repeated until the drinker triumphs. When the drinker does succeed, they are given the dice and attempt to roll a seven, an eleven, or a double.

Play continues in this fashion until someone is successful in their roll, which initiates the challenge once again.

GAME OF SKILL · **GAME OF SKILL**

PYRAMID

A game where tactics and memory matter.

Number of Players
At least four

Type of Drink
This game requires concentration, so anything
stronger than beer might be dangerous

Additional Materials
A dining table
A deck of cards, possibly two
A sharp mind

Rules of the game

Pyramid begins with a pyramid of cards being laid face down on the table: one in the top row, two in the second row, three in the third row etc.

The pyramid can be as large as is desired, but there must be enough cards remaining for each player to be dealt four cards, the values of which they should keep hidden from the other players. A reserve deck to replace cards which are revealed during the game will also be needed.

Play commences with the flipping of the card at the top of the pyramid.

At any time, a player holding a card which matches the value of the most recently flipped card can choose another player and command them to pay a drinking fine. An example is that if a six were flipped, someone holding a six would be free to choose another player and command them to drink.

Pyramid is complicated by the inclusion of bluffs.

Each player is free to issue a command without holding an appropriate card.

If the player who is commanded accepts the command, he or she drinks as usual. If the player who is commanded decides to challenge the command, the player who issued the command must show their card. If the command is proven to be legitimate, the challenging player's fine is doubled. If the command is proven to be a bluff, the fine is doubled and rebounds upon the player who issued the command.

Once all fines have been paid, any cards which have been shown are replaced with fresh cards from the deck. Play continues with the next card being flipped, moving from left to right.

As play advances across and down the pyramid, drinking fines increase.

A fine incurred when play has reached the second row of cards is worth double that of a fine incurred while play is on the first row, for example. A fine incurred when play has reached the third row is worth triple that of a fine incurred while play is on the first row, etc. These increases are in addition to the rules already mentioned.

A player may command two or more people to drink at the turn of a particular card, but must be able to back up their command with multiple cards of the appropriate denomination.

An example is that if, at the turn of a jack, a player commands two people to drink, they must be able to show two jacks if challenged or must pay the appropriate fine.

Tactics and memory are very important in Pyramid. It is vital to be able to remember which cards have already been drunk upon, in order to work out who is lying and who is telling the truth.

Naturally, this becomes increasingly difficult as play progresses and players' brains become befuddled with alcohol!

Pyramid comes with a number of variations. Beeramid asks players to look at their cards only once before being placed face down upon the table. Play continues in the usual fashion, but if someone is challenged they must be able to pick out the appropriate card from the selection lying face down in front of them. Failure to do so, even if the player actually holds the appropriate card, results in double the fine rebounding upon the player who issued the command.

Also, jokers may be included in the game. If a joker is revealed in the pyramid a player can command everyone else in the game to pay a drinking fine.

If the player who issued the command is successfully challenged, however, all the fines rebound upon that player (singly, rather than doubly, to give the player some chance of surviving the evening).

GAME OF CHANCE

THE SIMPSONS

GAME OF CHANCE

Mmmmmm beer!

Number of Players
Unlimited

Type of Drink
Anything: beer, wine, whatever
takes the participants' fancy

Additional Materials
A television
A recording of *The Simpsons* or access to a channel
showing episodes of *The Simpsons*

31

Rules of the game

This is an egalitarian game, because everyone drinks at the same time.

If one or more of the players are particularly hardcore, they might like to drink spirits while other folk drink less potent beverages.

Basically, when any one of the following conditions is met by the appropriate character, each player drinks.

Of course, players are free to invent their own rules to give this game a personal touch.

Homer
- says "D'oh!"
- eats donuts
- drools
- says "mmm... (insert name of food etc. here)"

Marge
- kisses Homer
- growls at Homer
- her hair casts a gigantic shadow

Bart
- makes a prank phone call
- says "eat my shorts"

Lisa
- mentions humanity
- plays the saxophone

Maggie
- falls over etc. etc.

GAME OF SPEED

MURUER!

GAME OF SPEED

Have you ever played Wink Murder?

Number of Players

This game really needs a large group, eight people or more,
to work effectively.

Type of Drink

Whatever you like

Additional Materials

A decent space—a large living room or something similar
As many playing cards as there are players,
including one ace and one king

34

Rules of the game

To begin the game, players stand in a circle. The cards are shuffled and one card is dealt to each player.

Whoever is dealt the king becomes the detective and stands in the middle of the circle; whoever is dealt the ace becomes the murderer but keeps this information a secret.

The murderer's aim is to kill off the other players by winking at them. When a player is winked at, they "die" (murder offers the potential for some particularly theatrical deaths) and pay a small drinking fine for having failed to evade the killer.

The detective, meanwhile, attempts to discover who the murderer is.

If the detective guesses successfully, the murderer pays a medium-sized drinking fine and a fresh round of play begins.

If the detective guesses incorrectly, they pay a medium-sized drinking fine and play continues. If the murderer manages to massacre every civilian in the room, the detective who failed to unmask the killer pays a large drinking fine.

GAME OF CHANCE

◈ QUEENS ◈

GAME OF CHANCE

The beauty of this game is its simplicity—but beware the fourth queen!

Number of Players
At least four

Type of Drink
Spirits and mixers

Additional Materials
A pack of playing cards

Rules of the game

It works most effectively when played in a bar or at the home of someone with a well-stocked drinks cabinet, because it requires a selection of spirits and mixers.

Players sit around a table and the cards are dealt, one at a time, face up. Whoever is dealt the first queen selects a spirit; whoever receives the second selects a mixer.

The recipient of the third queen buys (or makes) the chosen concoction and the person who is dealt the final queen is expected to drink it.

Of course, players can create hideous mixtures, but such a strategy can easily backfire.

A variation on this game is played with the player who is dealt the first queen choosing a beer and the player who is dealt the second choosing a shot. This, too, can lead to some nightmare drinking experiences.

Does anyone fancy an Irish Stout with a tequila chaser?

GAME OF SKILL
GAME OF SKILL

✤ **STAR WARS** ✤

This game can last all night, so is ideal for hardened drinkers.

Number of Players

As many as you like (and can fit in your living room)

Type of Drink

Whatever you desire and plenty of it

Additional Materials

A working TV

A working VCR/DVD player

A copy of episodes IV-VI of *Star Wars* on video/DVD

Rules of the game

Of course, players are free to stop the game after one or two movies, or at any time they feel sick! Below is a long list of events to look out for during the movies; the skill element lies in keeping your eyes peeled for them.

When they occur, each player takes a sip of their drink (or more where indicated). Here we go:

- Someone has a bad feeling about this
- It's their only hope
- An entire planet is described as having a uniform climate
- Someone is choked

- A female other than Princess Leia is on screen
- An old Jedi (including Darth) begins rambling about the Force
- Someone loses a hand
- A remarkable work of technology explodes in a single blast
- There is a tremor in the force
- Someone is absolved of blame ("it's not my/your fault!")
- One or more of our heroes narrowly escape being munched by a monster

- A Jedi is far more powerful than he appears

- Someone yells "No!"

- Someone does something which appears crazy, but which proves successful (Double for anyone other than Han)

- Someone appears in all three movies wearing the same outfit

- A Jedi uses the power of mind control

- Folk kiss

- A hero appears dressed in white or a villain appears dressed in black

- Double if the scenario is reversed (a hero in black etc., only the first person on screen if there are many at one time)

- Triple if someone torn between the light and the dark wears gray

- If you find yourself conversing with the characters

- An alien who has clearly spent many hours in make-up vanishes without saying a word

- Someone (or something) attempts to extract money from Han

- A ship which has been hit rockets out of control and crashes into something

- A light saber is used

- Something is Luke's destiny

- Luke moans about something

- Luke discovers a long-lost relative

- Luke fights a monster or some sort of alien

- Luke demonstrates his acrobatic prowess

- Luke narrowly avoids being swallowed up by a chasm

- Luke appears upside down

- Luke and Lando appear in the same location at the same time

- Double if they deign to converse with one another

- Luke's parentage is foreshadowed

- Luke refuses stubbornly to accept advice

- Luke yells "Artoooooo!"

- Leia is rude to someone

- Leia wears an outfit which covers her entire body except her face and hands

- Double when she wears her gold bikini

- Obi Wan makes a cameo after his death

- Han boasts about the *Millennium Falcon*

- Someone is insulting towards the *Falcon*

- Some component fails on the *Falcon*

- Double if the hyperdrive fails

- Yoda's grammar escapes him

- Yoda talks Yodaese

- R2-D2 undergoes some horrible disaster
- R2-D2's head spins wildly
- C-3PO loses some part of his anatomy
- Double if he is totally dismembered
- C-3PO enumerates the number of forms of communication with which he is familiar
- A Rebel pilot or co-pilot comes from an ethnic minority
- Double if they are an alien
- A Rebel pilot says "Nice shot..."
- A Rebel pilot says "I've been hit..."
- Tarkin boasts of the Death Star
- That stormtrooper knocks his head

That's the lot, though of course players are free to add their own rules and/or ignore these suggestions.

GAME OF SKILL

I HAVE NEVER

GAME OF SKILL

This game requires honesty and can be very revealing...

Number of Players

Best played with a small number of intimate friends
(or total strangers if you're a real extrovert)

Type of Drink

It's a personal choice with this game

Additional Materials

An enquiring mind
A willingness to reveal dark secrets

Rules of the game

Players sit around a table or on the floor (the latter can help to create an appropriate atmosphere of intimacy) and whoever feels inclined pipes up with a true negative statement about themselves.

If anyone else in the group has done what the speaker disavows, that person simply drinks.

To begin with, statements tend to be fairly tame, such as "I have never been to London" or "I have never danced the tango."

As the game progresses, however, and people grow more confident the alcohol-fueled, statements tend to become more explicit.

This can be great fun, and can also lead to a good deal of embarrassment on the part of anyone who drinks to a statement such as "I have never hung naked out of a bedroom window..."

LIAR! LIAR!

❖   ❖

**This game requires a watchful eye
and a good deal of cunning to play well.**

Number of Players

Six or fewer

Type of Drink

Beer or wine for each player, some monstrous
concoction for the loser to drink as a fine

Additional Materials

A deck of playing cards

46

Rules of the game

The cards are dealt face down until the deck is empty, with each player receiving approximately the same number of cards.

Play begins with the player to the dealer's left laying cards face down in the center of the table (or on the floor) and naming the cards they lay. For example, someone could lay down two cards and claim that they are two threes. If the player is believed, play continues with each player required to lay cards in sequence.

In this example, the next player would be required to lay down at least one three, or at least one four.

Should anyone be suspected of lying, they can be accused with the cry "Liar, Liar." Their cards are flipped, and if they are found to be lying they pay a drinking fine and collect all the cards from the middle.

If they have been accused falsely, however, the player who made the accusation is fined and collects the cards.

Play continues until all the players except one have managed to lay down all their cards, at which point the losing player drinks whatever cocktail has been created for the purpose.

MATCHBOX

**Players are seated around a table,
each with a drink of their own.**

Number of Players

Enough to make a good group,
at least four

Type of Drink

Anything which is drunk out
of tall glasses

Additional Materials

A matchbox

Rules of the game

Play commences with one person throwing the matchbox. Play revolves around the collection and payment of fines, which are accrued as follows: if the matchbox lands on its side, two "fingers" of beer are added to the tally; if it lands on its end, four fingers are added. If the matchbox lands flat, the thrower pays whatever fine has been accrued.

Therefore, fines are only paid when the matchbox lands flat, allowing for the possibility of huge fines being built by skillful players.

There are a few extra fines which can be invoked in Matchbox, to catch out the careless or thoroughly soused player. If any matches fall out of the box, a fine equal to one finger for each escaped match is paid.

If the box is thrown clear of the table, a fixed two-finger penalty is enforced. Should the box be thrown into the player's own drink, the player is required to finish the drink and replenish their glass.

Finally, if the box is thrown into someone else's drink, the player who made the throw drains the drink and buys another for the victim.

GAME OF CHANCE

DERBY DAY

GAME OF CHANCE

Derby Day brings all the fun of the races
into your very own living room.

Number of Players
At least four

Type of Drink
Something sophisticated, perhaps

Additional Materials
A deck of playing cards
A long table to serve as a race track
Counters of some sort (matches etc.)

Rules of the game

Well, the stakes might be smaller, but the principle is the same. Each player begins with the same number of counters. Twenty, perhaps, or fifty if this is going to be a full program of racing.

In addition, a bank is set up from which to pay winning gamblers and store the lost stakes of those poor fools who bet on a nag.

Before the racing can commence, the course must be marked, which involves removing all the kings and queens from the pack and placing them in a line, head to tail. These denote the eight spaces along which the "horses" will compete. The horses themselves are the aces, which are lined up at one end of the table, ready to make their way down the course.

Each player bets as many counters as they desire on the horse of their choice, and the race begins. Players can bet on multiple horses, improving their chances both of winning and of drinking.

The cards, which must be well shuffled, are flipped one by one. Whichever suit the flipped card belongs to, the corresponding horse moves one space along the course, accompanied by the frenzied cries of the race commentator.

Play continues in this manner, with the winning horse being the first one to move past the finishing line (i.e. when nine cards of its suit have been flipped).

At this stage, anyone who bet on the winning horse is rewarded with double their original stake from the bank. Everyone else loses their stake to the bank. Also, losing gamblers pay a drinking fine. This is calculated by multiplying the number of spaces their horse is from the finishing line by the number of counters they staked upon its success.

An example: *if someone staked three counters on a heart, and the horse finished three spaces from the finishing line, the player would pay a nine-sip drinking fine.*

Once all fines have been paid, the next race can be started.

Derby Day comes with a multitude of variations:

• Firstly, two decks of cards can be used, offering the possibility of a race of double the length.

• Secondly, players may bet on a horse to win, place (finish first or second), or show (finish first, second or third).
This is a relatively safe bet, but with fewer rewards. If the bet is successful, the player receives only their stake plus one counter in return. If the player's bet fails, however, and their horse finishes last, the drinking fine is doubled. In these circumstances, by the way, two horses tied for second both place, two horses tied for third

both show, and three horses tied for second all place.

There are also several possibilities regarding the counters. Some people might like to use them simply as a means of determining who has played most successfully during the evening. More mercenary players might like to make the betting genuine and expect people to pay to be included in the game, with counters exchanged for cash at the end of the evening.

A slightly more genteel possibility is that counters entitle those who hold them to ask other players to pay drinking fines.

For example, someone with four spare counters can give them to someone else on condition that the recipient drinks four sips of their drink. Players may well wish to evolve their own rules to Derby Day, in addition to those listed here.

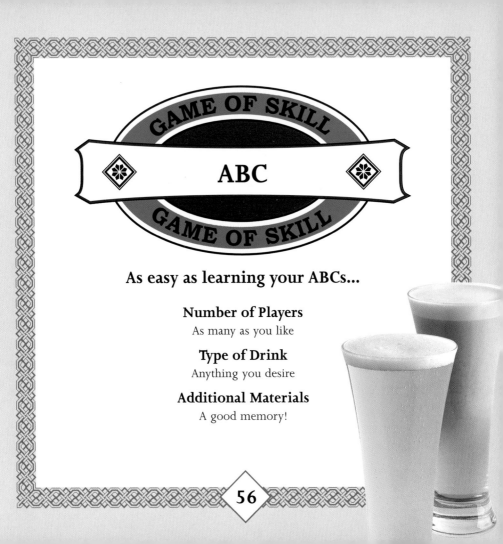

GAME OF SKILL

ABC

GAME OF SKILL

As easy as learning your ABCs...

Number of Players
As many as you like

Type of Drink
Anything you desire

Additional Materials
A good memory!

Rules of the game

ABC is basically a game of memory, in which a group of people sit in a circle, or around a table, and challenge each other to memorize words in sequence.

Someone starts the game by stating a letter of the alphabet and a noun which begins with that letter.

For example, the first player could say, "A is for avocado." The second player takes up the game by repeating what the first player said and adding to it, using the next letter of alphabet. In this example, the second player could say, "A is for avocado, B is for badger."

Following from the second player, the third might add, "A is for avocado, B is for badger, C is for calculator."

Play continues in this fashion, with players fined for speaking out of turn, missing out letters or hesitating unduly.

By the time the alphabet is halfway through, this game usually becomes a real mindbender.

GAME OF SPEED

❖ FIZZ BUZZ ❖

GAME OF SPEED

Fizz Buzz is acknowledged as an all-time classic drinking game.

Number of Players
Works well with a group of
around five or six

Type of Drink
Can be played with anything

Additional Materials
Some mathematical ability

Rules of the game

This game is extremely simple to play but very difficult to master.

Play begins with the players seated in a circle on the floor or around a table, this time calling out numbers in sequences. The first player, therefore, would call out the number one; the second player would call out the number two, etc.

Complications occur because any number which is a multiple of five, or which features the digit five, must be replaced by the word "buzz." Also, any number which is a multiple of seven, or which features the digit seven, is replaced by the word "fizz." Thus, the opening stretch of the game will run as follows: one; two; three; four; buzz; six; fizz.

Players are fined for failure to say the appropriate number, "buzz," or "fizz," where appropriate.

Fines may also be introduced for players who hesitate unduly. This game becomes more fun as higher numbers are reached and players are required to keep track mentally of the buzzing and fizzing (when the numbers being called out are in the fifties, for example). Numbers can, of course, be replaced by both "buzz" and "fizz": fifty-seven would become "buzz fizz" and seventy "fizz buzz."

Twenty-ones

Fizz Buzz is closely related to Twenty-ones, which involves more complicated rules and a rather different objective.

In Twenty-ones, the fizzing and buzzing are dropped. Instead, players are free to call out one, two, or three numbers at a time. If they call out one number, play continues in sequence; two numbers, the direction of play reverses. If they call out three numbers, play continues in the same direction with the next player in the sequence skipped over.

Anyone who makes a mistake pays a drinking fine and recommences play from the number one.

If the number twenty-one is reached successfully, the player who finds him or herself saying "twenty-one" pays a large drinking fine.

However, this is compensated for by the opportunity to invent a new rule. For example, the player might choose to swap the numbers three and eight, causing a sequence to run thus: one; two, eight (play reverses); four; five, six, seven (next player skipped); three, nine (play reverses), etc.

Once several rules are in place, and players are somewhat inebriated, this game can be hilarious. What's more, the possibility of reaching twenty-one can soon disappear into the ether!

GAME OF CHANCE

❋ SNAKES AND LADDERS ❋

GAME OF CHANCE

Do you remember playing Snakes and Ladders as a child?

Number of Players
Up to four

Type of Drink
Any are suitable, cocktails liven up the proceedings

Additional Materials
A copy of the Snakes and Ladders board game

62

Rules of the game

This game makes use of the board game which is probably somewhere in your attic.

The game is set up as usual, with each player choosing a counter and rolling the dice. Play continues in this fashion until someone lands upon either a snake or a ladder.

If a player lands on a ladder, that player counts how many squares they are propelled by the ladder on the following basis: number of squares up the board plus number of squares across the board. If the player moves three squares upward and two across, for example, that equates to five fingers of drink. The player is then entitled to ask any one of the other players to pay a drinking fine equivalent to the result of the calculation.

When someone lands on a snake, of course, the calculation is reversed. The number of squares the player moves across the board is added to the number of squares they move downward, and the player pays the drinking fine.

Players might like to invent additional rules, allowing the person who wins a game to mix cocktails with which to play the next round, for example.

GAME OF SKILL

THE JUG GAME

GAME OF SKILL

This is a fun game with a
little skill attached.

Number of Players
Four or more

Type of Drink
Beer, in a jug or you can
use tall glasses if playing with lightweights!

Additional Material
The capacity to drink a lot of beer
A tactical mind

64

Rules of the game

Play commences with a group of people sharing a jug of beer.

The jug is passed from one person to another, with each person drinking as much or as little as they want to.

The twist is that the person who takes the penultimate swig from the jug is expected to buy the next one, leading to some tactical play.

Do you try to finish the jug when it is still fairly full, risking failure and leaving someone else with an easy finish?

Alternatively, do you leave as much as possible in the jug, assuming that the next player will not be able to finish it?

This tactic, of course, can be dangerous if the player to your left possesses the ability to drink a small Eastern European army under the table.

65

BEER ROULETTE

This is similar to Russian roulette but a little less dangerous!

Number of Players

Six, ideally, to match the number who play real Russian roulette

Type of Drink

Beer, all of the same brand, in cans

Additional Materials

A sense of humor
A towel might be useful

Rules of the game

With players sitting around a table, the cans are gathered together and one is shaken up hard enough to ensure it will spray beer all over the place when opened.

The selection of cans is then shuffled thoroughly, thus hiding from the players which can contains the fizzy beer (this, of course, is the reason why the cans need to be of the same brand).

Players take it in turns to open a can, pointing it directly at their own face. Of course, one of the cans will deposit its contents all over the person who opens it, leaving them soggy, bedraggled, and smelling like a cheap bar.

Everyone else is free to sigh with relief and finish their beer. As some compensation, the player who has been sprayed is given the opportunity of shaking up the next can in order to begin the following round.

JAMES BOND

**Never mind a license to kill,
this game is a permit to drink.**

Number of Players
As many as wish to participate

Type of Drink
Martini, shaken not stirred

Additional Materials
A working television and VCR/DVD player
A copy of a James Bond movie on video/DVD

Rules of the game

For added absurdity, players might like to be wearing tuxedos, making this a good game to play before a ball or some other formal event.

Like *The Simpsons* and *Star Wars*, this game involves people drinking in accordance with the action on screen, so the possibilities are infinite.

Here are a few suggestions of moments at which to drink:

- When someone says "James"
- When someone says "Bond"
- When someone says "James Bond"
- When James is referred to using an assumed surname
- When a villain reveals his plan for world domination
- When a woman catches James' eye across a crowded bar/casino /mosque, etc.
- When a woman James has slept with proves to be in league with a villain
- When Q says "Be careful, 007"
- When James uses a gadget Q has given him
- When James is in bed with a woman and M calls him on the phone
- When a woman says something along the lines of "James, do you have to go?"

GAME OF SPEED

DRUG DEALER

GAME OF SPEED

**A very simple game,
and not as dangerous as it sounds.**

Number of Players
At least four, but no real limit

Type of Drink
Beer

Additional Materials
A deck of cards

72

Rules of the game

It's okay, there are no illegal narcotics in this game, but if played well you will be reaching for some aspirin in the morning.

You take as many cards from a deck as there are players in the game, but make sure you only have one ace and one king.

Shuffle the cards and deal them out, the player who gets the ace is the drug dealer; the person with the king is the policeman.

The drug dealer then winks discreetly at the other players until one of them notices the wink. They then call out, "The deal is done."

The policeman then has to guess who is the drug dealer.

For every wrong guess he has to drink for five seconds. But if the policeman sees the wink, the drug dealer has to drink for five seconds.

Once the dealer's identity has been revealed, the cards can be shuffled and dealt again for a new round, and so on.

GAME OF SPEED

BOAT RACE

GAME OF SPEED

Don't worry, you don't need a boat to play this game!

Number of Players

At least four, but unlimited except that
you must have even numbers

Type of Drink

Beer

Additional Materials

Some space
A broom handle (optional extra for the more adventurous)

Rules of the game

In a boat race, each team works in unison to achieve their goal. The bigger men will help out the cox, who in turn helps them by steering the boat…

And the same principle applies here. The "teams" line up with beers in hand, standing and all facing the same direction.

On the command "Quaff" the first person throws back their beer as quickly as possible. When this is completed the emptied glass is put on top of their head. The process then continues down the line until the last person.

Speed is the key to this game and if a team is falling behind, any member of the "crew" can, instead of drinking their beer, simply empty its contents over their head.

To add extra spice to the game, when each member finishes their beer they could run a few paces, place their forehead on top of a broom handle and run around it three times. Sit back and enjoy the comic results, but remember it's your go next!

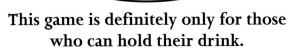

GAME OF SKILL

❖ WITHNAIL & I ❖

GAME OF SKILL

**This game is definitely only for those
who can hold their drink.**

Number of Players

Can be played solo, but not advised

Type of Drink

Anything with alcohol

Additional Materials:

A copy of the film *Withnail & I*
A meat pie
Cake • Access to medical help

Rules of the game

If you haven't seen this film, it's a British classic starring Richard E. Grant and Paul McGann.

It tells the story of two "resting actors" who spend most of their time drinking when they decide that they need a break in the country. This trip inevitably ends up in an almighty bender.

The idea is that you match them drink for drink, drinking when they do as the film progresses.

Here's what you will have to consume:

1. A quarter bottle of wine

2. A gin, a cider with ice and a meat pie

3. Lighter fluid (**BUT PLEASE DON'T!** Substitute with gin or vodka)

4. Several large sherries

5. Red wine

6. Whisky

7. Port

8. More whisky and "a pair of pints"

9. More sherry

10. "The finest wines known to man" and "cake"

11. Another whisky

12. Château Margaux 1953

STRIPTEASE

This is a great way to get to know people very quickly!

Number of Players
An even amount of men and women

Type of Drink
Whatever you fancy, but spirits get people into the mood more quickly

Additional Materials
A pair of dice

78

Rules of the game

Each person takes a turn at rolling the dice.

If an even number shows the person takes a drink. If an odd number appears they have to remove an item of clothing.

It can be that simple, but you can add the "doubles rule" to make things more interesting.

1-1—it's the thrower's choice, a drink or a piece of clothing.

2-2—the person to the right of you has to drink.

3-3—you get to do nothing.

4-4—someone of your choice has to tell a truth or perform a dare.

5-5— another piece of good luck, you get to put back on an item of clothing.

6-6—you get to kiss the person on your right.

A useful tip for this game is to put on extra items of underwear!

BATTLESHIP

This is a game for the nautical adventurers amongst you.

Number of Players

At least four, but as many as you like really

Type of Drink

beer

Additional Materials

A jug and a smaller glass that will fit inside it

80

Rules of the game

This game offers the chance to re-enact the British Navy's epic search for the sinker of *HMS Hood*, the mighty German battleship, *Bismarck*.

Although exactly how the *Bismarck* was sunk is still a matter of debate amongst military historians, this alcohol-fueled re-enactment doesn't rely upon historical accuracy! Unsurprisingly perhaps, it's more a test of your drinking ability.

Fill the jug three-quarters full of beer and then place the glass inside it.

You need to make sure it doesn't sink; you can add a small amount of beer to the glass to help balance it.

Then each person has to add a small amount of beer to the glass, making sure they don't sink it. However, the laws of physics cannot be held at bay for too long and when that fateful last drop of beer is added, the person who sunk the glass must drink the entire contents of the jug and glass.

GAME OF SKILL

OPERATION

GAME OF SKILL

You may need to make a trip to the attic before starting this game.

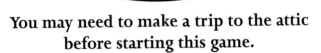

Number of Players
Four or more

Type of Drink
Your choice, but this game can get very messy with spirits

Additional Materials
The board game Operation—and don't forget the batteries!

82

Rules of the game

If you were lucky enough to have had this game when you were a kid, then it's time to get it out from the attic and blow off the dust.

It helps with the fun if you've had a few drinks already; this is a test of your dexterity, don't forget!

The game is played in the normal fashion: you're given an operation to perform and you try to do it in the usual way.

But instead of taking the money as a prize there's drink to be had. If you get it right and remove his heart successfully, everyone has to have five drinks, if you get it wrong you have to consume the five drinks.

Obviously, as the night wears on, the hands will get more and more unsteady and competitors more and more loaded!

GAME OF CHANCE

BEER TENNIS

GAME OF CHANCE

You don't need to follow tennis to understand this game.

Number of Players
At least two

Type of Drink
Cans or bottles of beer of different sizes

Additional Materials
A strong bladder

Rules of the game

You don't need to use a racket in this version of tennis; here small beers count as individual games, large ones as sets.

You score according to the number of games and sets you can consume. After five small beers you must consume a large one to take the set.

Whenever you go to the bathroom you lose two games. You are competing both against yourself and for best scoreline so the more comfort breaks you take the more likely you are to run out the loser. If your scoreline is 6-0, 6-0, 6-0 and your opponent's 6-0, 6-0,

6-2, then you are entitled to declare yourself the winner!

You'll probably be able to take the first two sets without too much trouble, but the third may well be a very tough battle. Make sure you win the third though, because realistically speaking, it would be foolish to try to win a fourth!

GAME OF SPEED

CATEGORIES

GAME OF SPEED

You might want to prepare a specialist subject to win at Categories.

Number of Players
You should try to get at least five to make this work best

Type of Drink
Your favorite beer

Additional Materials
Good general knowledge

Rules of the game

Like all the best drinking games this is simple and, therefore, really effective.

A person names a category and then everyone else has to name a different thing from that category.

The round ends when a person can't think of something to add, hesitates too long or repeats something someone has already said. They then have to drink their forfeit and come up with a new category.

Unless you're in a really vindictive mood it's best to have a subject that most people have some knowledge of. Presidents of the USA is a good one, but left-handed European golfers is best left to the experts.

GAME OF SPEED

POWER HOUR

GAME OF SPEED

This one's only for the hardest of hardened drinkers.

Number of Players
Unlimited

Type of Drink
Beer

Additional Materials
A clock or watch with a second hand

Rules of the game

This is a game that really can sort the men from the boys. As the name suggests, it is for the power drinkers amongst us.

To start the game each person pours themselves a glass of beer. About half a glass is best; a full tall glass would be bordering on suicidal!

At the start of the minute, each person drinks their beer and then fills their glass up to the same level ready to repeat the process at the start of the next minute. This sounds easy, doesn't it?

However, after the fifth or sixth minute you will begin to feel the pace.

The aim is to complete the "Power Hour." If you fail to drink and refill within a minute, you're out.

Remember, this challenge is complicated by the toilet rule. Any trip to the toilet means you're out of the game.

A word of warning:
It doesn't take a genius to work out that completing the "Power Hour" would involve consuming sixty drinks, a feat that would actually prove dangerous. We therefore recommend that you don't put this game into practice but instead enjoy its theoretical perfection while sitting back and savoring your drink.

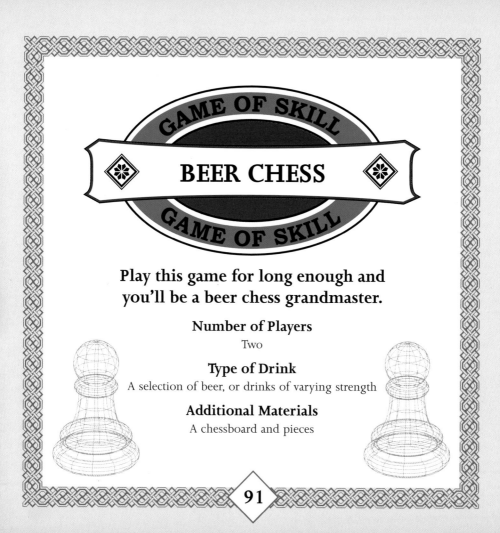

GAME OF SKILL

❖ BEER CHESS ❖

GAME OF SKILL

Play this game for long enough and you'll be a beer chess grandmaster.

Number of Players
Two

Type of Drink
A selection of beer, or drinks of varying strength

Additional Materials
A chessboard and pieces

Rules of the game

Beer Chess is played in the same way as normal chess, but as you have probably worked out, you have to consume alcohol as the game develops.

The first thing to sort out is which drink will represent which piece on the board. Traditionally, the drink is stronger for the more valuable pieces with the king at the top of the list.

The sensible way to play would be to have one type of alcohol, such as beer, with varying strengths. Alternatively, you could choose different types of spirits in shot glasses and mix your drinks like mad!

Here are some suggestions:

Pawns—lager

Rooks—beer

Knights—cider

Bishops—wine

Queen—spirits

King—cocktails

Once your drinks have been established the rules look like this:

1. If you move a piece, you must take a sip from the corresponding drink.

2. If your piece is taken, you must gulp down the drink.

3. If you take a sip from a drink the relevant piece must be moved.

4. You can take as long as you want to finish a drink if you lose a piece, but if you lose another piece you have to finish the first drink in one.

5. If you get put in check, you must drink from the king.

6. Castling means drinking from the king and the rook.

7. If you are checkmated you must drink your king, the opponent's king and all of what's left of your pieces.

GAME OF SKILL

◈ DRINKER'S BLOCKS ◈

GAME OF SKILL

**Make sure it's not your
fault when the blocks tumble!**

Number of Players
As many as possible

Type of Drink
Beer

Additional Materials
A Jenga™ set or similar
A marker pen

94

Rules of the game

The appeal of building blocks, for most, stretches back to toddler days, but tower block games have undergone a revival in recent years. They have even started to appear in some bars in the form of large, communal sets.

Now here's a way of making your game a bit more fun. You take a marker pen and add various rules and penalties to each of your blocks.

These should include things like gulp down the communal drink, buy a drink for everyone, and perform a handstand, but generally the orders are up to you.

Once this has been done, the pieces are stacked in the usual way and the game begins as normal.

As each player takes a piece they must do what the order says. As you would expect, if all the pieces are knocked over the guilty party must finish their drink.

95

CARDINAL PUFF

Sucess depends on your powers of concentration.

Number of Players

This is best kept to a small group, four or five is best

Type of Drink

Any kind of beer works best for this

Additional Materials

A table

A head for numbers

Rules of the game

This game is all about concentration and the ability to spot a mistake from your opponents and then ruthlessly exploit it.

Everyone sits around a table and a volunteer starts the proceedings.

They stand up and with a full glass on the table say "Here's to the memory of Cardinal Puff."

They then tap the table with a finger of the left hand and then tap it again with a finger from the right hand. They must then tap their right leg with their right hand and then the left leg with the left hand.

Finally, they take a swig from their drink using only their forefinger and thumb to hold the glass. The turn then passes to the person to the right who must follow the same procedure but do it twice and take two drinks. The tally of taps then increases by the person.

Any mistake should be punished with a suitable drinking fine or dismissal from the game.

INDIAN POKER

In this version of poker, being dealer isn't necessarily an advantage.

Number of Players
At least five

Type of Drink
Beer

Additional Materials
A deck of cards

98

Rules of the game

If you've played High or Low, then you should take to this like a duck to water.

Each player is dealt a card from the deck but must not look at it. Instead it must be held against their forehead so that everyone else but the player in question can see it.

Everyone is given a minute or two to consider what cards are on show and plan their strategy.

The dealer then starts the betting by saying how many fingers of beer they want to wager on themselves having the highest card.

The others can fold at this stage if they feel they can't beat this, but they must drink whatever the largest bet was from their glass.

When everyone has made their bet, all cards are placed on the table. The one with the lowest card has to drink the total number of drinks bet—this can be very high.

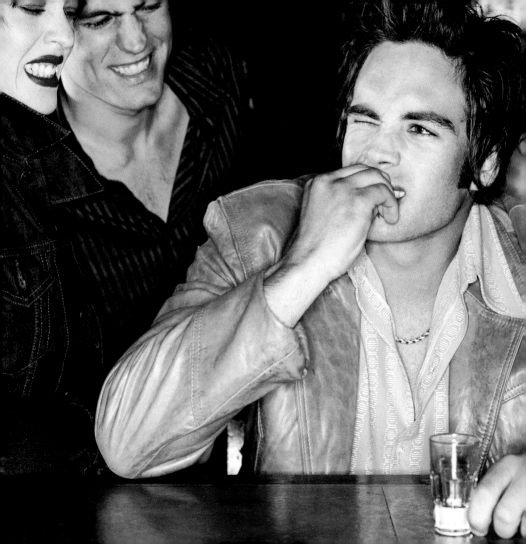

GAME OF SKILL

CHANDELIERS

GAME OF SKILL

This game came by its name only because
of the antics it once inspired.

Number of Players

Four

Type of Drink

Both beer and spirits can be used

Additional Materials

A table
Five glasses
A coin

Rules of the game

If you like exotic light fittings then this is the game for you. It combines accuracy with the ability to consume your drink at a potentially rapid rate.

One empty glass is placed in the middle of the table and the four others are placed around it in a kind of protective ring. Each one should be opposite a player.

The first player then tries to bounce a coin off the table and into one of the glasses.

If it goes into a glass it has to be filled with a drink of your choice. If you miss you have to take a five drinks penalty measure, one for each of the glasses on the table.

The turn then passes to the person on the right.

If the coin lands in a glass that is full, the person it faces has to drink the contents in one swig.

If the coin lands in the center glass, all four outer glasses are filled.

Then each player must put their hand flat on the table with their middle finger touching their glass.

When the person who bounced the coin in says "Go," everyone has to drink the contents of their glass.

The last one to finish has to fill the center glass immediately and drink that without any hesitation.

Players with particularly bad aim may find that swinging from a light fitting is a distinct possibility.

GAME OF SPEED

BARTENDER TEST

GAME OF SPEED

No bartender is going to thank you for this…

Number of Players
One player per bartender

Type of Drink
The whole top shelf is an option

Additional Materials
Help from your friends

Rules of the game

This is a game for those who are either very good drinkers or have been in the sun a bit too long.

It's very easy to play. First you go into a bar—one that is not too busy is best—and order a spirit.

You must then pay for this with a note large enough to make the bartender have to get you some change.

While he's doing this you must swig your drink ASAP. When the bartender returns with your change, order another spirit and pay with another large note. And so the game continues.

Now this challenge usually ends in one of three ways: one, you fall down drunk, which means you lose. Two, the bartender throws you out for being annoying which means no one wins.

Or finally, the bar shuts, you're still standing and you win. Either way, this game is not for the faint-hearted.

GAME OF SPEED

BUNNIES

GAME OF SPEED

This works best if you're not afraid to make a fool of yourself.

Number of Players
This can be played with limitless numbers, but about ten is ideal

Type of Drink
Beer

Additional Materials
A sense of humor

Rules of the game

The players sit around in a circle and someone usually volunteers to start the game.

They do this by assuming the bunny position. This involves placing their thumbs next to their temples and wiggling their fingers wildly.

The person sitting to their left immediately raises their right hand to their temple and wiggles their fingers.

The person on the right does the same with their left hand. Everyone else in the circle must keep their hands by their sides.

Now the fun begins. The bunny has then to flick his hands off his temple and point to another player, who must immediately assume the bunny position, with their neighbors helping them along.

During the changeover, the bunny can feint, and if a person's hands move they have to pay a penalty.

You can look ridiculous playing this game, so maybe it's one to be played at home!

BAR GOLF

As with real golf, you have to avoid water to win.

Number of Players
Two or more

Type of Drink
It's up to you...

Additional Materials
Eighteen bars close together

Rules of the game

Most golfers call the bar the nineteenth hole, so this game was invented by way of a thank you for that compliment.

You need to have eighteen bars close together for this game to work well.

The aim is to play each bar like a hole on the golf course, with the lowest score at the end of the round being the winner.

How do you score the game? Every bar is par four and the drink you consume dictates what score you get at each one.

An eagle is two shots under par and is achieved by gulping down a neat double spirit.

A birdie is one under par and is scored by drinking a spirit and a mixer. A beer will only get you par, a small beer will leave you one over par and a non-alcoholic drink will land you a two over par double bogey.

The temptation is to go for a lot of doubles, but this can lead to trouble by the thirteenth as you begin to realize you've drunk the best part of a bottle of vodka.

The winner is the person with the lowest score, but can anyone last the course?

GAME OF SKILL

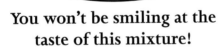

❖ CEMENT MIXER ❖

GAME OF SKILL

You won't be smiling at the taste of this mixture!

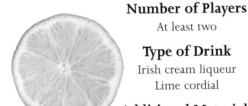

Number of Players
At least two

Type of Drink
Irish cream liqueur
Lime cordial

Additional Materials
A strong stomach

Rules of the game

The Cement Mixer is a shooter drink that is very popular in bars today. This game takes that concept one step further.

Each person in the game puts a double shot of Irish cream liqueur in their mouth, followed by a double shot of lime cordial—be sure not to swallow either liquid.

Everyone then has to shake their head from side to side as quickly as possible.

Very soon everyone will realize that a nasty metamorphosis is happening in their mouth. What can only be described as a lump of cheese will be forming and it won't be a pleasant-tasting piece of cheddar!

The winner of this game is the last person shaking their head without swallowing their exciting new cocktail.

GAME OF CHANCE

MAVERICK

GAME OF CHANCE

This is a type of roulette, but it will be the room spinning not the wheel after a few games.

Number of Players
Six to eight people works best

Type of Drink
Vodka

Additional Materials
Four shot glasses if you have six people, five if you have seven etc.

Rules of the game

Roulette was one of the movie character Maverick's favourite games. Like the game of roulette, the object of this game is to choose the winning number or in this case, person.

One person in the group is chosen as "Maverick," the other players have a shot glass put in front of them. Then one glass is filled with vodka, the others with water. Maverick has to leave the room and the glasses are moved around . All the other players then gulp down their drinks. Maverick then returns to the room and has to guess which person drank the vodka.

Opinion is split on how you can do this. Smelling the breath can be allowed but these are rules that should be decided by the house before the game begins. If Maverick guesses right, all the other players have to take a shot and the person who had the vodka becomes Maverick. If Maverick gets it wrong he has to take the shot and guesses again.

FLIP THE CUP

❖ ❖

A simple, but potentially frustrating game.

Number of Players
An even number of people to form two teams

Type of Drink
Beer

Additional Materials
Plastic cups
A table

Rules of the game

Begin this game by splitting the players into two teams. It's better to get an even split in terms of drinking capabilities in each team as this makes the game work better.

The two teams line up at one end of the table. The first person on each side then has to run to the other end of the table and drink the contents of their plastic cup.

Now comes the tricky part. They then have to turn the cup upside down with one side hanging over the edge of the table.

Now each player has to put their finger inside the cup and try to flip it over so it lands back on its bottom, ready to be refilled.

This is not as easy as it sounds. When this has been successfully done, the cup is filled and the next team member tries their luck.

The winning team is the first to have all its members complete the challenge.

GAME OF SPEED

BOUNCING BALL

GAME OF SPEED

A tricky game which can
easily leave you confused.

Number of People
Four or more

Type of Drink
Beer or spirits

Additional Materials
An imaginary ball
A great deal of concentration

Rules of the game

This game can appear to the uninitiated to be really easy. All you have to remember are three words: whiz, bounce, and boing. What could be complicated about that?

The challenge comes when you have to remember what each one means as it's shouted out so you can follow the path on the imaginary ball and "catch it" when your turn comes.

Whiz means that the "ball" passes to the person next to you.

Bounce means that it has to move past the next person and arrive in the hands of the second person along.

Boing means the ball must change direction and go back the other way.

Any mistakes or hesitations are punishable by a drinking fine.

117

GAME OF SPEED
GOLF BALL GAME
GAME OF SPEED

A rather less genteel version of the game.

Number of Players
No limits

Type of Drink
Beer

Additional Materials
A golf ball

Rules of the game

This game already has a legendary reputation and it is well deserved because it's a classic.

All you need is a room full of players with beers in their hands and one person with a golf ball in their hand.

The aim of the game is to drop the ball into someone's glass, at which point they have to drink the contents without question or hesitation.

But then hunted becomes the hunter as it is now their turn to try to deposit the ball. The real skill of the game is to make sure you put the ball into a fresh drink, making sure your victim has to swig as much as possible. Another favorite tactic is to get the same person repeatedly.

It's amazing what several beers drunk in an hour can do to a person. You'll soon realize the reason why the more experienced players hold their glasses with a finger across the top.

This is undoubtedly one of the best drinking games there is.

GAME OF SKILL

❖ FREEMASONS' CLUB ❖

GAME OF SKILL

**One of the simplest games ever devised,
it has only one rule.**

Number of Players
At least four, but as many as you want really

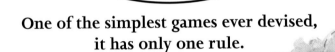

Type of Drink
Anything you choose

Additional Materials
Sharp eyesight

Rules of the game

Before you start rolling up one trouser leg and putting on funny little aprons this has got nothing to do with secret societies.

The only ritual this involves is having a laugh with your friends and drinking buddies.

The game is unique in that it only has one rule, which is no drinking with your right hand.

The game begins when someone suggests that the lodge should hold a meeting. That means that the only rule is in play. If someone is caught drinking with their right hand they must finish their drink. The punishment is the same if you accuse someone of right-handed drinking when it was their left.

The good thing about this game is that it has a gentle pace and can last all night. But as the evening progresses the chances of a penalty increase.

GAME OF CHANCE

PEANUT DERBY

GAME OF CHANCE

Now you can have a gamble
every time you go to the bar.

Number of Players
Two

Type of Drink
Beer

Additional Materials
Half a peanut for each player

123

Rules of the game

The Kentucky Derby is an annual event where almost everyone in the country usually has a bet. Now you can enjoy a gamble whenever you go to the bar.

Every person in the race orders a beer from the bar and then takes their nut of choice in their hand. Then on the command "and they're off" everyone drops their nut into their glass. The nut will sink to the bottom of the glass, before rising back to the top. The person whose nut is the last one back to the top, has to gulp down their beer, nut and all, in one.

"Experts" have discussed the relative strengths of the salted versus the dry roasted and the cashew versus the peanut for some time. Does the smoothness of the salted give it a more streamlined body in beer? Is your choice of beer important? Do the bubbles in lager add more zip compared to the more sedate appearance of strong beer? All these variables can only add to the excitement.

RING OF DEATH ❖

GAME OF CHANCE

Not as dangerous as it sounds... but almost!

Number of Players
Four

Type of Drink
Beer

Additional Materials
A deck of cards